Copyright © 2022 Kristen J. Lloyd

All rights reserved. No part of this book may be reproduced or used in any manner without the prior written permission of the copyright owner, except for the use of brief quotations in a book review.

Paperback: 978-0-578-26338-0

To request permissions, contact the publisher at
contact@kristenjlloyd.com

First Paperback edition March 2022

Editing: Susan Morris, Bob Morphis
Illustrations, story, and layout: Kristen J. Lloyd

Krazy AniTainment Inc.
P.O. Box 126
Midway UT 84049

KristenJLloyd.com

Dedicated to Honeybee
and my daughter Lilly.

A special thank you to Devin, Bob, and Susan for your help with proofing my story.

Also a big thank you to Devin, Lisa, Carlie, and Cameron for the extra play dates with Lilly so I could create this! Love you all.

Find Your Brave

Written and Illustrated by
Kristen J. Lloyd

Once there was a girl named Ani who lived on a farm.

She was also afraid of . . .

Aren't you afraid of falling?" Ani asked.

"A little," Honeybee replied, "but I think I will Find My Brave."

"How do you find that?" Ani Puzzled.

"By looking of course!" the calf mooed. "And by trying one scary thing at a time."

When the sun went down, Ani was afraid to walk to the house. It was too dark.

"Maybe you can pretend to be a star!" Honeybee said.

"A star? Why a star?" Ani asked.

"Stars like the dark because it helps them shine brighter," the calf replied.

"Maybe they can help you Find Your Brave!"

One day while Ani was fixing Honeybee's hair, a spider dropped down from the rafters in the barn. Ani screamed!

"He's so spooky!" She squeaked.

"But he is so cute! Honeybee mooed. "And tiny!"

Ani looked closer. "I guess he is tiny . . ."

". . . maybe he isn't so scary after all."

"See? Finding your Brave is fun."
Honeybee smiled.

One night they were watching the stars twinkle.

"What if I forget how to Find my Brave?" Ani asked.

"Maybe you can find a way to remember before you forget," Said Honeybee.

So Ani started to draw their Brave Adventures on paper.

And as their adventures grew, her collection of drawings did too.

It was fun to remember all of the times Honeybee helped her.

Until Ani remembered the drawings she had made of their adventures together.

Because Honeybee had helped her Find her Brave.

Kristen and Honeybee

The Children's book "Find Your Brave" is based on the real life relationship between Kristen J. Lloyd and her favorite milk cow Honeybee. Their bond helped Kristen through many challenges that she faced in life, and indeed helped her Find her Brave.

When her grandparents retired and sold the cows, Kristen was determined to keep Honeybee and take her to Utah with her. However, she realized that her new life wouldn't be best for Honeybee, and she made the difficult decision to let Honeybee go with the rest of the herd to their new home.

My Pal Moo

To cope with letting Honeybee go, Kristen began drawing cartoons of the two of them together that she called "My Pal Moo". It helped her feel connected to Honeybee, and sparked the idea of one day creating a children's book.

When Kristen's original song "My Brave" started to gain a fanbase after its release in 2018, it sparked the idea to combine the "Brave" concept from the song with her experiences and cartoons of Honeybee. It became a wonderful opportunity to help others learn to be Brave through art as well as through music.

"Outside Looking In" 2018

www.ingramcontent.com/pod-product-compliance
Lightning Source LLC
Chambersburg PA
CBHW040620010526

44109CB00036B/126